BATTLE AND OTHER POEMS

THE MACMILLAN COMPANY
NEW YORK · BOSTON · CHICAGO · DALLAS
ATLANTA · SAN FRANCISCO

MACMILLAN & CO., LIMITED
LONDON · BOMBAY · CALCUTTA
MELBOURNE

THE MACMILLAN CO. OF CANADA, LTD.
TORONTO

BATTLE

AND OTHER POEMS

BY

WILFRID WILSON GIBSON

AUTHOR OF "DAILY BREAD," "FIRES," "BORDERLANDS
AND THOROUGHFARES," ETC.

New York

THE MACMILLAN COMPANY

1916

TO MY WIFE

CONTENTS

BATTLE

CONTENTS

FRIENDS

STONEFOLDS

BATTLE

BEFORE ACTION

I sit beside the brazier's glow,
And, drowsing in the heat,
I dream of daffodils that blow
And lambs that frisk and bleat—

Black lambs that frolic in the snow
Among the daffodils,
In a far orchard that I know
Beneath the Malvern hills.

Next year the daffodils will blow,
And lambs will frisk and bleat;
But I'll not feel the brazier's glow,
Nor any cold or heat.

BREAKFAST

We eat our breakfast lying on our backs,
Because the shells were screeching overhead.
I bet a rasher to a loaf of bread
That Hull United would beat Halifax
When Jimmy Stainthorpe played full-back
    instead
Of Billy Bradford. Ginger raised his head
And cursed, and took the bet; and dropt
    back dead.
We eat our breakfast lying on our backs,
Because the shells were screeching overhead.

THE BAYONET

This bloody steel
Has killed a man.
I heard him squeal
As on I ran.

He watched me come
With wagging head.
I pressed it home,
And he was dead.

Though clean and clear
I've wiped the steel,
I still can hear
That dying squeal.

THE QUESTION

I wonder if the old cow died or not.

Gey bad she was the night I left, and sick.

Dick reckoned she would mend.   He knows a
    lot—

At least he fancies so himself, does Dick.

Dick knows a lot.   But maybe I did wrong

To leave the cow to him, and come away.

Over and over like a silly song

These words keep bumming in my head all
    day.

And all I think of, as I face the foe

And take my lucky chance of being shot,

Is this—that if I'm hit, I'll never know

Till Doomsday if the old cow died or not.

THE RETURN

He went, and he was gay to go;
And I smiled on him as he went.
My son—'twas well he couldn't know
My darkest dread, nor what it meant—

Just what it meant to smile and smile
And let my son go cheerily—
My son . . . and wondering all the while
What stranger would come back to me.

SALVAGE

So suddenly her life
Had crashed about that grey old country
    wife,
Naked she stood, and gazed
Bewildered, while her home about her blazed,
New-widowed, and bereft
Of her five sons, she clung to what was left,
Still hugging all she'd got—
A toy gun and a copper coffee-pot.

DEAF

This day last year I heard the curlew calling
By Hallypike
And the clear tinkle of hill-waters falling
Down slack and syke.

But now I cannot hear the shrapnel's scream-
ing,
The screech of shells:
And if again I see the blue lough gleaming
Among the fells

Unheard of me will be the curlew's calling
By Hallypike
And the clear tinkle of hill-waters falling
Down slack and syke.

MAD

Neck-deep in mud,
He mowed and raved—
He who had braved
The field of blood—

And as a lad
Just out of school
Yelled: "April fool!"
And laughed like mad.

RAINING

The night I left my father said:
"You'll go and do some stupid thing.
You've no more sense in that fat head
Than Silly Billy Witterling.

"Not sense to come in when it rains—
Not sense enough for that, you've got.
You'll get a bullet through your brains,
Before you know, as like as not."

And now I'm lying in the trench
And shells and bullets through the night
Are raining in a steady drench,
I'm thinking the old man was right.

[17]

SPORT

And such a morning for cubbing—
The dew so thick on the grass!
Two hares are lolloping just out of range
Scattering the dew as they pass.

A covey of partridge whirrs overhead
Scatheless, and gets clean away;
For it's other and crueller, craftier game
We're out for and after to-day!

THE FEAR

I do not fear to die
'Neath the open sky,
To meet death in the fight
Face to face, upright.

But when at last we creep
In a hole to sleep,
I tremble, cold with dread,
Lest I wake up dead.

IN THE AMBULANCE

"Two rows of cabbages,
Two of curly-greens,
Two rows of early peas,
Two of kidney-beans."

That's what he is muttering,
Making such a song,
Keeping other chaps awake,
The whole night long.

Both his legs are shot away,
And his head is light;
So he keeps on muttering
All the blessed night.

"Two rows of cabbages,
Two of curly-greens,
Two rows of early peas,
Two of kidney-beans."

HILL–BORN

I sometimes wonder if it's really true
I ever knew
Another life
Than this unending strife
With unseen enemies in lowland mud,
And wonder if my blood
Thrilled ever to the tune
Of clean winds blowing through an April noon
Mile after sunny mile
On the green ridges of the Windy Gile.

THE FATHER

That was his sort.
It didn't matter
What we were at
But he must chatter
Of this and that
His little son
Had said and done:
Till, as he told
The fiftieth time
Without a change
How three-year-old
Prattled a rhyme,
They got the range
And cut him short.

THE REEK

To-night they're sitting by the peat
Talking of me, I know—
Grandfather in the ingle-seat,
Mother and Meg and Joe.

I feel a sudden puff of heat
That sets my ears aglow,
And smell the reek of burning peat
Across the Belgian snow.

NIGHTMARE

They gave him a shilling,
They gave him a gun,
And so he's gone killing
The Germans, my son.

I dream of that shilling—
I dream of that gun—
And it's they that are killing
The boy who's my son.

COMRADES

As I was marching in Flanders
A ghost kept step with me—
Kept step with me and chuckled
And muttered ceaselessly:

"Once I too marched in Flanders,
The very spit of you,
And just a hundred years since,
To fall at Waterloo.

"They buried me in Flanders
Upon the field of blood,
And long I've lain forgotten
Deep in the Flemish mud.

"But now you march in Flanders,
The very spit of me;
To the ending of the day's march
I'll bear you company."

THE LARK

A lull in the racket and brattle,
And a lark soars into the light—
And its song seems the voice of the light
Quelling the voices of night
And the shattering fury of battle.

But again the fury of battle
Breaks out, and he drops from the height—
Dead as a stone from the height—
Drops dead, and the voice of the light
Is drowned in the shattering brattle.

THE VOW

Does he ever remember,
The lad that I knew,
That night in September
He vowed to be true—

Does he hear my heart crying
And fighting for breath
In the land where he's lying
As quiet as death?

MANGEL–WURZELS

Last year I was hoeing,
Hoeing mangel-wurzels,
Hoeing mangel-wurzels all day in the sun,
Hoeing for the squire
Down in Gloucestershire
Willy-nilly till the sweaty job was done.

Now I'm in the 'wurzels,
In the mangel-wurzels,
All day in the 'wurzels 'neath the Belgian
    sun.
But among this little lot
It's a different job I've got—
For you don't hoe mangel-wurzels with a
    gun.

HIS FATHER

I quite forgot to put the spigot in.
It's just come over me. . . .   And it is queer
To think he'll not care if we lose or win
And yet be jumping-mad about that beer.

I left it running full.   He must have said
A thing or two.   I'd give my stripes to hear
What he will say if I'm reported dead
Before he gets me told about that beer!

HIT

Out of the sparkling sea
I drew my tingling body clear, and lay
On a low ledge the livelong summer day,
Basking, and watching lazily
White sails in Falmouth Bay.

My body seemed to burn
Salt in the sun that drenched it through and
    through
Till every particle glowed clean and new
And slowly seemed to turn
To lucent amber in a world of blue. . . .

I felt a sudden wrench—
A trickle of warm blood—
And found that I was sprawling in the mud
Among the dead men in the trench.

BACK

They ask me where I've been,
And what I've done and seen.
But what can I reply
Who know it wasn't I,
But someone just like me,
Who went across the sea
And with my head and hands
Killed men in foreign lands. . . .
Though I must bear the blame
Because he bore my name.

HIS MATE

"Hi-diddle-diddle
The cat and the fiddle" . . .

I raised my head,
And saw him seated on a heap of dead,
Yelling the nursery-tune,
Grimacing at the moon. . . .

"And the cow jumped over the moon.
The little dog laughed to see such sport
And the dish ran away with the spoon."

And, as he stopt to snigger,
I struggled to my knees and pulled the
    trigger.

THE DANCERS *characteristic*

All day beneath the hurtling shells
Before my burning eyes
Hover the dainty demoiselles—
The peacock dragon-flies.

Unceasingly they dart and glance
Above the stagnant stream—
And I am fighting here in France
As in a senseless dream—

A dream of shattering black shells
That hurtle overhead,
And dainty dancing demoiselles
Above the dreamless dead.

THE JOKE

He'd even have his joke
While we were sitting tight,
And so he needs must poke
His silly head in sight
To whisper some new jest
Chortling, but as he spoke
A rifle cracked. . . .
And now God knows when I shall hear the
rest!

CHERRIES

A handful of cherries
She gave me in passing,
The wizened old woman,
And wished me good luck—

And again I was dreaming,
A boy in the sunshine,
And life but an orchard
Of cherries to pluck.

THE HOUSEWIFE

She must go back, she said,

Because she'd not had time to make the bed.

We'd hurried her away

So roughly . . . and, for all that we could
    say,

She broke from us, and passed

Into the night, shells falling thick and fast.

VICTORY

I watched it oozing quietly
Out of the gaping gash.
The lads thrust on to victory
With lunge and curse and crash.

Half-dazed, that uproar seemed to me
Like some old battle-sound
Heard long ago, as quietly
His blood soaked in the ground.

The lads thrust on to victory
With lunge and crash and shout.
I lay and watched, as quietly
His life was running out.

THE MESSAGES

"I cannot quite remember. . . . There were
  five
Dropt dead beside me in the trench—and
  three
Whispered their dying messages to me. . . ."

Back from the trenches, more dead than
  alive,
Stone-deaf and dazed, and with a broken
  knee,
He hobbled slowly, muttering vacantly:

"I cannot quite remember. . . . There were
  five
Dropt dead beside me in the trench, and three
Whispered their dying messages to me. . . .

"Their friends are waiting, wondering how
    they thrive—

Waiting a word in silence patiently. . . .

But what they said, or who their friends
    may be

"I cannot quite remember. . . . There were
    five

Dropt dead beside me in the trench,—and
    three

Whispered their dying messages to me. . . ."

THE QUIET

I could not understand the sudden quiet—
The sudden darkness—in the crash of fight,
The din and glare of day quenched in a
    twinkling
In utter starless night.

I lay an age and idly gazed at nothing,
Half-puzzled that I could not lift my head;
And then I knew somehow that I was lying
Among the other dead.

FRIENDS

TO THE MEMORY OF
RUPERT BROOKE

He's gone.

I do not understand.

I only know

That as he turned to go

And waved his hand

In his young eyes a sudden glory shone:

And I was dazzled by a sunset glow,

And he was gone.

23d April, 1915

RUPERT BROOKE

I

Your face was lifted to the golden sky
Ablaze beyond the black roofs of the square
As flame on flame leapt, flourishing in air
Its tumult of red stars exultantly
To the cold constellations dim and high:
And as we neared the roaring ruddy flare
Kindled to gold your throat and brow and
    hair
Until you burned, a flame of ecstasy.

The golden head goes down into the night
Quenched in cold gloom—and yet again you
    stand
Beside me now with lifted face alight,

As, flame to flame, and fire to fire you burn. . . .
Then, recollecting, laughingly you turn,
And look into my eyes and take my hand.

II

Once in my garret—you being far away
Tramping the hills and breathing upland air,
Or so I fancied—brooding in my chair,
I watched the London sunshine feeble and grey
Dapple my desk, too tired to labour more,
When, looking up, I saw you standing there
Although I'd caught no footstep on the stair,
Like sudden April at my open door.

Though now beyond earth's farthest hills
    you fare,
Song-crowned, immortal, sometimes it seems
    to me

That, if I listen very quietly.
Perhaps I'll hear a light foot on the stair
And see you, standing with your angel air,
Fresh from the uplands of eternity.

III

Your eyes rejoiced in colour's ecstasy,
Fulfilling even their uttermost desire,
When, over a great sunlit field afire
With windy poppies streaming like a sea
Of scarlet flame that flaunted riotously
Among green orchards of that western shire,
You gazed as though your heart could never
    tire
Of life's red flood in summer revelry.

And as I watched you, little thought had I
How soon beneath the dim low-drifting sky

Your soul should wander down the darkling
    way,
With eyes that peer a little wistfully,
Half-glad, half-sad, remembering, as they see
Lethean poppies, shrivelling ashen grey.

IV

October chestnuts showered their perishing
    gold
Over us as beside the stream we lay
In the Old Vicarage garden that blue day,
Talking of verse and all the manifold
Delights a little net of words may hold,
While in the sunlight water-voles at play
Dived under a trailing crimson bramble-spray,
And walnuts thudded ripe on soft black
    mould.
Your soul goes down unto a darker stream

FRIENDS

Alone, O friend, yet even in death's deep
    night
Your eyes may grow accustomed to the dark
And Styx for you may have the ripple and
    gleam
Of your familiar river, and Charon's bark
Tarry by that old garden of your delight.

WILLIAM DENIS BROWNE

(Gallipoli, 11th June, 1915)

Night after night we two together heard
The music of the Ring,
The inmost silence of our being stirred
By voice and string.

Though I to-night in silence sit, and you,
In stranger silence, sleep,
Eternal music stirs and thrills anew
The severing deep.

TENANTS

Suddenly, out of dark and leafy ways,
We came upon the little house asleep
In cold blind stillness, shadowless and deep,
In the white magic of the full moon-blaze:
Strangers without the gate, we stood agaze,
Fearful to break that quiet, and to creep
Into the house that had been ours to keep
Through a long year of happy nights and
    days.

So unfamiliar in the white moon-gleam,
So old and ghostly like a house of dream
It seemed, that over us there stole the dread
That even as we watched it, side by side,
The ghosts of lovers, who had lived and died
Within its walls, were sleeping in our bed.

SEA–CHANGE

Wind-flicked and ruddy her young body
   glowed
In sunny shallows, splashing them to spray:
But when on rippled silver sand she lay,
And over her the little green waves flowed,
Coldly translucent and moon-coloured showed
Her frail young beauty, as if rapt away
From all the light and laughter of the day
To some twilit, forlorn sea-god's abode.

Again into the sun with happy cry
She leapt alive and sparkling from the sea,
Sprinkling white spray against the hot blue sky,
A laughing girl . . . and yet, I see her lie
Under a deeper tide eternally
In cold moon-coloured immortality.

GOLD

All day the mallet thudded, far below
My garret, in an old ramshackle shed
Where ceaselessly, with stiffly nodding head
And rigid motions ever to and fro
A figure like a puppet in a show
Before the window moved till day was dead,
Beating out gold to earn his daily bread,
Beating out thin fine gold-leaf blow on blow.

And I within my garret all day long
To that unceasing thudding tuned my song,
Beating out golden words in tune and time
To that dull thudding, rhyme on golden rhyme.
But in my dreams all night in that dark shed
With aching arms I beat fine gold for bread.

[52]

THE OLD BED

Streaming beneath the eaves, the sunset light
Turns the white walls and ceiling to pure gold,
And gold, the quilt and pillows on the old
Fourposter bed—all day a cold drift-white—
As if, in a gold casket glistering bright,
The gleam of winter sunshine sought to hold
The sleeping child safe from the dark and cold
And creeping shadows of the coming night.

Slowly it fades: and stealing through the gloom
Home-coming shadows throng the quiet room,
Grey ghosts that move unrustling, without
    breath,
To their familiar rest, and closer creep
About the little dreamless child asleep
Upon the bed of bridal, birth and death.

[53]

TREES

(To Lascelles Abercrombie)

The flames half lit the cavernous mystery
Of the over-arching elm that loomed profound
And mountainous above us, from the ground
Soaring to midnight stars majestically,
As, under the shelter of that ageless tree
In a rapt dreaming circle we lay around
The crackling faggots, listening to the sound
Of old words moving in new harmony.

And as you read, before our wondering eyes
Arose another tree of mighty girth—
Crested with stars though rooted in the earth,
Its heavy-foliaged branches, lit with gleams
Of ruddy firelight and the light of dreams—
Soaring immortal to eternal skies.

OBLIVION

Near the great pyramid, unshadowed, white,
With apex piercing the white noon-day blaze,
Swathed in white robes beneath the blinding
rays
Lie sleeping Bedouins drenched in white-hot
light.
About them, searing to the tingling sight,
Swims the white dazzle of the desert ways
Where the sense shudders, witless and adaze,
In a white void with neither depth nor height.

Within the black core of the pyramid
Beneath the weight of sunless centuries
Lapt in dead night King Cheops lies asleep:
Yet in the darkness of his chamber hid
He knows no black oblivion more deep
Than that blind white oblivion of noon skies.

COLOUR

A blue-black Nubian plucking oranges
At Jaffa by a sea of malachite
In red tarboosh, green sash, and flowing white
Burnous—among the shadowy memories
That haunt me yet by these bleak Northern
    seas
He lives for ever in my eyes' delight,
Bizarre, superb in young immortal might—
A god of old barbaric mysteries.

Maybe he lived a life of lies and lust:
Maybe his bones are now but scattered dust:
Yet, for a moment he was life supreme
Exultant and unchallenged: and my rhyme
Would set him safely out of reach of time
In that old heaven where things are what they
    seem.

NIGHT ✔

Vesuvius, purple under purple skies
Beyond the purple, still, unrippling sea;
Sheer amber lightning, streaming ceaselessly
From heaven to earth, dazzling bewildered
    eyes
With all the terror of beauty: thus day dies
That dawned in blue, unclouded innocency;
And thus we look our last on Italy
That soon, obscured by night, behind us lies.

And night descends on us, tempestuous night,
Night, torn with terror, as we sail the deep;
And like a cataract down a mountain-steep
Pours, loud with thunder, that red perilous
    fire. . . .
Yet shall the dawn, O land of our desire,
Show thee again, re-orient, crowned with light!

humor

THE ORPHANS

At five o'clock one April morn
I met them making tracks,
Young Benjamin and Abel Horn,
With bundles on their backs.

Young Benjamin is seventy-five,
Young Abel, seventy-seven—
The oldest innocents alive
Beneath that April heaven.

I asked them why they trudged about
With crabby looks and sour—
"And does your mother know you're out
At this unearthly hour?"

They stopped: and scowling up at me
Each shook a grizzled head,
And swore; and then spat bitterly,
As with one voice they said:

"Homeless, about the country-side
We never thought to roam;
But mother, she has gone and died,
And broken up the home."

?

Mooning in the moonlight
I met a mottled pig,
Grubbing mast and acorn,
On the Gallows Rigg.

"Tell, oh tell me truly,
While I wander blind,
Do your peepy pig's eyes
Really see the wind—

"See the great wind flowing
Darkling and agleam
Through the fields of heaven
In a crystal stream?

[60]

"Do the singing eddies
Break on bough and twig
Into silvery sparkles
For your eyes, O pig?

"Do celestial surges
Sweep across the night
Like a sea of glory
In your blessed sight?

"Tell, oh tell me truly!"
But the mottled pig
Grubbing mast and acorns,
Did not care a fig.

THE PESSIMIST

His body bulged with puppies—little eyes
Peeped out of every pocket, black and bright;
And with as innocent, round-eyed surprise
He watched the glittering traffic of the night.

"What this world's coming to I cannot tell,"
He muttered, as I passed him, with a whine—
"Things surely must be making slap for hell,
When no one wants these little dogs of mine."

THE SWEET–TOOTH

Taking a turn after tea
Through orchards of Mirabelea
Where clusters of yellow and red
Dangled and glowed overhead,
Who should I see
But old Timothy,
Hale and hearty as hearty could be—
Timothy under a crab-apple tree.

His blue eyes twinkling at me,
Munching and crunching with glee
And wagging his wicked old head,
"I've still got a sweet-tooth," he said,
"A hundred and three
Come January,
I've one tooth left in my head," said he—
Timothy under the crab-apple tree.

GIRL'S SONG ✓

I saw three black pigs riding
In a blue and yellow cart—
Three black pigs riding to the fair
Behind the old grey dappled mare—
But it wasn't black pigs riding
In a gay and gaudy cart
That sent me into hiding
With a flutter in my heart.

I heard the cart returning,
The jolting jingling cart—
Returning empty from the fair
Behind the old jog-trotting mare—
But it wasn't the returning
Of a clattering, empty cart
That sent the hot blood burning
And throbbing through my heart.

[64]

THE ICE–CART

Perched on my city office-stool,
I watched with envy, while a cool
And lucky carter handled ice. . . .
And I was wandering in a trice,
Far from the grey and grimy heat
Of that intolerable street,
O'er sapphire berg and emerald floe,
Beneath the still, cold ruby glow
Of everlasting Polar night,
Bewildered by the queer half-light,
Until I stumbled, unawares,
Upon a creek where big white bears
Plunged headlong down with flourished heels
And floundered after shining seals
Through shivering seas of blinding blue.
And as I watched them, ere I knew,

I'd stripped, and I was swimming, too,

Among the seal-pack, young and hale,

And thrusting on with threshing tail,

With twist and twirl and sudden leap

Through crackling ice and salty deep—

Diving and doubling with my kind,

Until, at last, we left behind

Those big, white, blundering bulks of
    death,

And lay, at length, with panting breath

Upon a far untravelled floe,

Beneath a gentle drift of snow—

Snow drifting gently, fine and white,

Out of the endless Polar night,

Falling and falling evermore

Upon that far untravelled shore,

Till I was buried fathoms deep

Beneath that cold white drifting sleep—

Sleep drifting deep,
Deep drifting sleep. . . .

The carter cracked a sudden whip:
I clutched my stool with startled grip,
Awakening to the grimy heat
Of that intolerable street.

TO E. M.

(In memory of R. B.)

The night we saw the stacks of timber
    blaze
To terrible golden fury, young and strong
He watched between us with dream-dazzled
    gaze
Aflame, and burning like a god of song,
As we together stood against the throng
Drawn from the midnight of the city ways.

To-night the world about us is ablaze
And he is dead, is dead. . . . Yet, young
    and strong
He watches with us still with deathless gaze

TO E. M.

Aflame, and burning like a god of song,
As we together stand against the throng
Drawn from the bottomless midnight of hell's
    ways.

10th June, 1915.

MARRIAGE

Going my way of old
Contented more or less
I dreamt not life could hold
Such happiness.

I dreamt not that love's way
Could keep the golden height
Day after happy day,
Night after night.

ROSES

Red roses floating in a crystal bowl
You bring, O love; and in your eyes I see,
Blossom on blossom, your warm love of me
Burning within the crystal of your soul—
Red roses floating in a crystal bowl.

FOR G.

All night under the moon
Plovers are flying
Over the dreaming meadows of silvery light,
Over the meadows of June
Flying and crying—
Wandering voices of love in the hush of the
　　night.

All night under the moon,
Love, though we're lying
Quietly under the thatch, in silvery light
Over the meadows of June
Together we're flying—
Rapturous voices of love in the hush of the
　　night.

HOME

I

RETURN

Under the brown bird-haunted eaves of thatch
The hollyhocks in crimson glory burned
Against black timbers and old rosy brick,
And over the green door in clusters thick
Hung tangled passion-flowers, when we re-
    turned
To our own threshold: and with hand on latch
We stood a moment in the sunset gleam
And looked upon our home as in a dream.

Rapt in a golden glow of still delight
Together on the threshold in the sun
We stood rejoicing that we two had won

To this deep golden peace ere day was done,

That over gloomy plain and storm-swept
    height

We two, O love, had won to home ere night.

II

CANDLE–LIGHT

Where through the open window I could see

The supper-table in the golden light

Of tall white candles—brasses glinting bright

On the black gleaming board, and crockery

Coloured like gardens of old Araby—

In your blue gown against the walls of white

You stood adream, and in the starry night

I felt strange loneliness steal over me.

You stood with eyes upon the candle flame

That kindled your thick hair to burnished gold,

As in a golden spell that seemed to hold
My heart's love rapt from me for evermore. . . .
And then you stirred, and opening the door,
Into the starry night you breathed my name.

III

FIRELIGHT

Against the curtained casement wind and sleet
Rattle and thresh, while snug by our own fire
In dear companionship that naught may tire
We sit,—you listening, sewing in your seat,
Half-dreaming in the glow of light and heat,
I reading some old tale of love's desire
That swept on gold wings to disaster dire
Then sprang re-orient from black defeat.

I close the book, and louder yet the storm
Threshes without. Your busy hands are still;

And on your face and hair the light is warm,
As we sit gazing on the coals' red gleam
In a gold glow of happiness, and dream
Diviner dreams the years shall yet fulfil.

IV

MIDNIGHT

Between the midnight pillars of black elms
The old moon hangs, a thin, cold, amber flame
Over low ghostly mist: a lone snipe wheels
Through shadowy moonshine, droning: and
    there steals
Into my heart a fear without a name
Out of primæval night's resurgent realms,
Unearthly terror, chilling me with dread
As I lie waking wide-eyed on the bed.

And then you turn towards me in your sleep
Murmuring, and with a sigh of deep content

HOME

You nestle to my breast; and over me

Steals the warm peace of you; and, all fear
    spent,

I hold you to me sleeping quietly,

Till I, too, sink in slumber sound and deep.

STONEFOLDS*

The ragged heather-ridge is black
Against the sunset's frosty rose;
With rustling breath, down syke and slack,
The icy, eager north-wind blows.

It shivers through my hair, and flicks
The blood into my tingling cheek;
And with adventurous urging pricks
My spirit, that in drowsy reek

Of glowing peats had dreamt too long,
Crouched in the cosy ingle-nook,
Till life seemed vainer than the song
The kettle sings upon the crook—

Till life seemed vainer than the puff
Of steam that perished in hot air—
A fretful fume, a vapour stuff
Of gusty passion, cloudy care.

But as, once more, I watch the stars
Re-kindle in the glittering west,
Beyond the fell-top's naked scars,
Life rouses in me with new zest.

The immortal wakens in my blood
Beneath the wind's relentless thresh;
And universal life at flood
Breaks through the bonds of bone and flesh.

I scale the utmost peak of night,
The eternal breath upon my face;
Till, borne on plumes of singing light,
I lose myself in starry space.

STONEFOLDS

Persons:

NICHOLAS THIRLWALL, an old shepherd.

RACHEL THIRLWALL, his wife.

RUTH THIRLWALL, his daughter.

RALPH MOORE, a young shepherd,

Nicholas' nephew.

Scene: The living-room of Stonefolds, a shep-herd's house on the fells. A door opens on to the yard, another to the back of the house. Nicholas, an infirm, old man, sits on the settle by the peat-fire with his back to the outer door. His wife, Rachel, moves about putting things away in a cupboard, tending the fire, &c. A clock in the corner ticks loudly. Storm rages without.

NICHOLAS.

Is Ralph there?

RACHEL.

                Nay, he's gone back to the fold.

NICHOLAS.

If only I might go with him! It's strange
The year's lambs should be born, and I not
    there.
The labouring ewes will miss my hand to-
    night;
Though Ralph's a careful fellow, he is young;
And six-and-fifty lambings have I seen.
It's hard, it's hard that I sit crippled here
When there's so much to do—so much to do!
That I, who should be tending the young lambs,
As helpless as a yeanling crouch and shake
Beside the peats, and shudder at the night.

RACHEL.

It's a wild night! See how beneath the door
The snow has silted. It's a perilous night
For young things to be born. Hark to the wind!

NICHOLAS.
Ay, it's the lambing-storm.

RACHEL.

               I'll set a pan
Of milk upon the hob, for Ralph may bring
Some motherless lamb to tend before the fire.

NICHOLAS.
It's hard, it's hard that all may help but me—
While I have seen so many young things born,
So many perish in my time. Worn out,
Useless and old, I sit before the fire
Warming my hands that once were never cold,
And now are never warm. I sit and shake

[83]

Like quaking-grass, and cannot even rise
To shift my seat, or turn my hand to aught,
When there's so much to do.
(*A noise as of someone knocking the snow off his
boots against the threshold.*)

What's that?

RACHEL.

It's Ralph.

(*The door opens, and Ralph comes in, white with
snow, carrying a lanthorn, and a new-born lamb
wrapped in his plaid. He looks about him, as
though expecting to see someone with Nicholas and
Rachel; then, with a sigh, he sets down the lanthorn on the table, and carries the lamb to the
hearth, and lays it on the rug before the fire, while
Rachel fills a bottle with warm milk.*)

RALPH.

The old lame ewe is dead. I've brought her lamb

[84]

To lie before the fire; but it is weak
And like to die.

NICHOLAS.

        Had I but tended her!

RALPH.

The ewe was old.

NICHOLAS.

        Ay, ay, the ewe was old,
And so must die, and none pay any heed!
I, too, am old—I, too, am growing old.

RALPH, *to Rachel, who is kneeling by the lamb.*

You keep the yeanling warm till I come back,
I doubt that it can live; but I must go.

        (*Takes his lanthorn and goes out.*)

RACHEL.

Ralph's a good lad and has a tender heart.

NICHOLAS.

Ay, he's a careful fellow. He should wed.

At his age I'd been wed hard on a year.

RACHEL.

But Ralph will never wed.

NICHOLAS.

      Why should he not?

He is a likely lad. Why should he not?

RACHEL.

It's just a year to-night since Ruth left home.

NICHOLAS.

Ruth! What of Ruth? The lass has made her
 bed,

And she must lie upon it now.

RACHEL.

     Poor Ruth!

Yet, Ralph will never wed.

NICHOLAS.

How can you tell?

RACHEL.

I watch him as he sits before the fire
Each night in his own corner, with still eyes
That gaze and gaze into the glowing peats
Until they burn as fiercely as the flame
On which they feed; and sometimes, suddenly,
His fingers grip the settle till it shakes;
And when I speak he heeds not, till the light
Has perished from his eyes, and, dull as ash,
They look upon the crumbling peats once
    more.

NICHOLAS.

A woman's fancies! Ralph is not a boy
To peak and pine because a silly wench,
Who, if she'd had but wit, might be his wife,
Flits one fine night. O Ruth! to give up Ralph

For that young wastrel, Michael! Ralph must
    wed
The sooner if he broods. A wife and babes
Will leave him little time for idle brooding.
He's not the fool his father was.

RACHEL.
                    Poor Ruth!
Yet, Ralph will never wed. At other times,
I see him sit and hearken all night long
As though he fretted for some well-known foot—
Listening with his whole body, like a hare—
Bolt-upright on the settle; every nerve
Astrain to catch the never-falling sound
Of home-returning steps. Only last night
I watched him till my heart was sore for him.
He seemed to listen with his very eyes,
That gleamed like some wild creature's.

             (*The clock strikes*.) It's gone ten.

[88]

Come, Nicholas, I will help you to your
bed.

NICHOLAS.

Nay, nay! I'll not to bed to-night. Why,
lass,
I have not gone to bed at lambing-time
Since I could hold a lanthorn! That must be
Nigh sixty years; and I'll not sleep to-night.
Though I be as much use asleep as waking
Since my legs failed me, yet, I could not sleep.
I can but sit and think about the lambs
That in the fold are opening wondering eyes,
Poor new-born things!

RACHEL.
                    This one lies very still.
I'll get more peats to heap upon the fire.
It's cold, maybe. (*Goes through the inner door.*)

[89]

NICHOLAS.

It's weak, and like to die.

(*The outer door slowly opens, and Ruth enters, wearily, with hesitating steps. She is dressed in a cloak, and is covered with snow. She pauses uncertainly in the middle of the room, and looks at her father, who, unaware of her presence, still sits gazing at the lamb, which opens its mouth as if to bleat, but makes no sound.*)

NICHOLAS.

Poor, bleating beast! We two are much alike,
At either end of life, though scarce an hour
You've been in this rough world, and I so long
That death already has me by the heels;
For neither of us can stir to help himself,
But both must bleat for others' aid. This world
Is rough and bitter to the newly born,
But far more bitter to the nearly dead.

RUTH, *softly.*

Father!

NICHOLAS, *not hearing her, and still mumbling to himself.*

I've seen so many young things born,
So many perish!
(*Rachel enters, and, seeing Ruth, drops the peats which she is carrying and folds her to her breast.*)

RACHEL.

Ruth! My child, my child!

NICHOLAS, *still gazing into the fire.*

Why harp on Ruth? The lass has made her
bed. . . .

RUTH, *tottering towards him and kneeling on the rug by his side.*

Father!

[91]

NICHOLAS.

> What, is it Ruth?   (*Fondling her.*)
>> My child, my child!

Why, you are cold; and you are white with
    snow!

You shiver, lass, like any new-born lamb.

(*Rachel meanwhile strips off Ruth's cloak, and fills
a cup with milk from the pan on the hob.*)

RUTH.

I thought I never should win home.   The snow

Was all about me.   Even now my eyes

Are blinded by the whirling white that stung

My face like knotted cords, and in my ears

Rustled of death—of cold, white, swirling death.

I thought I never should win home again

With that wild night against me. How I fought!

I was so weary, I was fain at whiles

To strive no more against the cruel night,

And could have lain down gladly in a drift,

As in my bed, to die . . . had I not
  known. . .

Yet, knowing, I dared not.   But I am dazed.

RACHEL, *holding the cup to Ruth's lips.*

Come, drink this milk.   'Twas heated for the
  lambs.

I little knew that for my own poor lamb

I set it on the hob an hour ago!

RUTH, *seeing for the first time the lamb on the
  hearth.*

The lambs?   I had forgotten—I am dazed.

This is the lambing-time; and Ralph . . .

              and Ralph . . .

NICHOLAS.

Is in the fold, where I should be if I . . .

Ruth, *bending over the lamb.*

Ah, what a night to come into the world!

Poor, motherless thing! and those poor, patient
    mothers!

I might have known it was the lambing-storm.

(*She moans and almost falls, but Rachel stays her
in her arms.*)

Rachel.

Child, you are ill!

Ruth.

Yes, I am near my time.

Rachel, *raising her from the ground and sup-
porting her.*

Come, daughter, your own bed awaits you now,

And has awaited you these many nights.

Come, Ruth.   (*They move slowly across the
    room.*)

[94]

Ruth.

      I thought I never should win home.

Nicholas, *as they pass into the inner room.*

Yes, I have seen so many young things born,

So many perish! Rachel! They are gone;

And we're alone again, the lamb and I.

Poor beast, poor beast, has she forgotten you

Now that her own stray lamb is home again?

You lie so still and bleat no longer now.

It's only I bleat now. Maybe, you're dead,

And will not bleat again, or need to bleat,

Because you're spared by death from growing

    old;

And it can scarce be long till death's cold clutch

Shall stop my bleating too.

(*He sits gazing into the fire, and dozes. Time
passes. The cry of a new-born babe is heard from
the next room.*)

NICHOLAS, *mumbling, half asleep.*

Yes, I have seen
So many young things born, so many perish!
(*He dozes again. After a while Rachel enters,
carrying a baby wrapped in a blanket, which she
lays on the rug before the fire.*)

RACHEL.
See, Nicholas! Wake up! It is Ruth's child.

NICHOLAS, *waking.*
Ruth's child! Why, Ruth is but a child herself!

RACHEL.
Don't sleep again, for you must watch the babe
While I go back to Ruth again. She lies
So still and cold; and knows naught of the child.
Unless she rouse, she cannot last till day.

(*Goes into the other room.*)
[96]

NICHOLAS.

So many young things perish; and I, so old,

Am left to sit all day with idle hands,

And can do naught to save them.

(*The knocking of snowy boots against the threshold is heard again. The door opens, and Ralph enters with his lanthorn.*)

Is that Ralph?

(*Ralph goes towards the lamb, but, seeing the child, stands gazing in amazement.*)

RALPH.

Uncle, what babe is this?

NICHOLAS.

Lad, Ruth is home.

RALPH.

Ruth has come home! I knew that she would

come.

She could not stay, though held so long from
  me,
For I have ever called her in my heart,
By day and night, through all the weary year.
I knew—I knew that she would come to-night
Through storm and peril, and within the fold
My heart has gone out to the labouring ewes,
And new-born lambs, and all weak, helpless
  things.
And yet I might have killed her!—though I
  sought
Only to draw her to my shielding breast.
She might have fallen by the way, and died,
On such a night! She shall not stray again.
The love that drew her from the perilous night
May never let her go.

(*Rachel, entering, is about to speak, but seeing
Ralph, pauses.*)

RALPH, *to Rachel.*
> Ruth has come home!

And we shall never let her go again.

RACHEL, *speaking slowly.*

Ay, Ruth is home.

(*Going to the hearth and taking the child in her arms.*)
> You poor, poor, motherless babe!

(*Ralph gazes at her as though stunned, then bends over the lamb.*)

RALPH.

It's dead. I must go back now to the fold.

I shall be there till morning.

> (*He crosses to the door and goes out.*)

RACHEL, *calling after him.*
> Ralph! your plaid!

(*She follows to the door and opens it. The snow drifts into the room.*)

RACHEL.

He's gone without his lanthorn and his plaid.

God keep him safe on such a night! Poor
Ralph!

Ruth's babe no longer breathes.

(*Laying the child by the dead lamb.*)

To-night has death

Shown pity to the motherless and weak,

And folded them in peace. How sweet they
sleep!

NICHOLAS.

We two have seen so many young things born,

So many perish; yet death takes us not.

Wife, bar the door; that wind blows through
my bones.

It's a long night. (*Clock strikes.*)

What hour is that?

[100]

Rachel.

It's one;
The night is over.

Nicholas.

Yet another day!

THE BRIDAL

Persons:

HUGH SHIELD, a young shepherd.

ESTHER SHIELD, his bride.

ANN SHIELD, his mother.

Scene: The living-room of Bleakridge, a lonely shepherd's cottage on the fells. In one corner is a four-post bed on which Ann Shield, an old, bed-ridden woman, lies sleeping, unseen behind the closed curtains. On the table in the middle of the room a meal is spread. The latch clicks, the door opens, and Hugh Shield enters, glancing towards the bed, then turns to hold open the door for Esther Shield, who follows him into the room.

HUGH.

Wife, welcome home!

(*Embracing her, and leading her to a chair.*)

Come, rest, for you are tired.

ESTHER.

No, I'm not weary.   (*Looking towards bed.*)

Does your mother sleep?

HUGH, *crossing to bed and peering betwixt the curtains.*

Ay, she sleeps sound, and we'll not waken her,
For she is ever fretful when she wakes.
It would not do to break the news . . .

ESTHER.

The news!
Did she not know we were to wed to-day?

HUGH.

She did not know I was to wed at all.

[103]

ESTHER.

Hugh! Why did you not tell her?

HUGH.

I don't know.

I would have told her when I spoke to you—
Just seven nights since—it seems so long ago!—
But when I breathed your name she put me off
Ere I had told my will. She's sorely failed,
And wanders in her speech. A chance word
    serves
To scare her like a shadow-startled ewe,
And send her old mind rambling through the
    past
Till I can scarce keep pace with her. Next
    morn
I spoke, and still she would not hear me out,
And yet she ever liked you, lass, and naught
She spoke against you; only her poor wits

Are like a flock of sheep without a herd;

And so she mumbled idle, driftless things;

Unless it were a mother's jealous fear

That made her cunning, and she sought to
    turn

My thoughts from you. Old people aye dread
    change.

ESTHER.

You should have told her ere we wedded, Hugh.

HUGH.

When I arose this morn, I went to her

To tell her, but she slept; and when I set

Her breakfast on the table by her bed,

I would have waked her, and stretched out my
    hand

To rouse her, and the words were on my lips;

And yet, I didn't touch her, spoke no word.

I was afraid to speak, I don't know why.
'Twas folly, lass, and yet I could not speak.

ESTHER.
You should have told her.

HUGH.
                        Well, it doesn't matter;
For we are wedded, Esther. I'm no boy,
That I must ever ask my mother's leave
Ere I do aught. I left her sleeping still;
And when she waked, she'd think me with the
    sheep;
And sup her meal in peace; and little know
Into what fold I wandered, and with whom!

ESTHER.
You should have told her, Hugh. She will be
    wroth

[106]

To wake and find you wed. If you were fright-
    ened
To tell her then, how will you tell her now?

HUGH.

'Twas not her wrath I feared. I scarce know
    why
I did not tell her; for I would have wed
Though she had bidden me "Nay" a thousand
    times.
Lass, do you think a word would hold me back,
Like a cowed collie, when I would be forth?
Not all the world could keep me from you, lass,
Once I had set my heart on you. D'you think
I should have taken "Nay," lass, even from you!

ESTHER.

Ay, you are masterful; and had your way
To church ere scarce I knew it; and, yet, Hugh,

You had not had your way so easily
Had it not been my way as well!

HUGH.

Ay, lass,
Naught could have held us from each other—
    naught;
And naught shall ever part us.

ESTHER, *glancing towards the bed*.

Hugh, she stirs.
Your voice has wakened her.

ANN, *from the bed*.
Hugh, are you there?

HUGH, *going towards the bed*.
Ay, mother.

ANN.

Lad, what hour is it?

[108]

HUGH.

Nigh noon.

ANN.

I did not wake till you had gone this morn.

I must have slumbered soundly, though I
slept

But little in the night. I could not sleep.

I lay awake, and watched the dark hours pass;

They seemed to trail as slowly as the years

On which I brooded, and did naught but brood,

Though my eyes burned for slumber—those
dark years

So long since passed! I did not sleep till dawn;

And then I dreamt again of those dark years;

And in my dream they seemed to threaten you.

And when I waked the clock was striking nine,

And you were gone. I must have slept again,

For you are here. I did not hear the latch.

HUGH.

Mother, I spoke to you the other eve

Of Esther—but you did not heed . . .

ANN.

My dream!

Hugh, lad, I heard your words with fearful
heart,

Yet, could not speak. Son, you must never
wed.

HUGH.

What say you, mother! Am I yet a boy—

A pup to bring to heel with "must" and
"shall"?

Mother, this cur's beyond your call!

ANN.

Nay, lad,

I don't bid you for bidding's sake; nor yet

Because I dread another mistress here.

Hugh, son, my mother's heart would **have**
    you wed;

Yet this same heart cries out to hinder **you**.

Believe me, for your happiness I speak.

You must not wed.

HUGH.

       Hush, mother! Don't speak now.

(*He motions to Esther, who comes forward to the
bed.*)

ANN, *turning towards Esther.*

Is someone there? You should have told me,
    Hugh.

Who is it, lad; for my old eyes are weak,

And the light dazzles them? I know the
    face.

Is't Esther Ord?

HUGH.

No, Esther Shield, my bride.

ANN, *after a pause.*

Then it's too late!   Had I but spoken
  then,

Or held my tongue for ever!

HUGH.

That were best.

Don't heed her, lass.   She doesn't know what
  she says.

ANN.

Would that I didn't know, had never known!

O son, it's you who do not know.   But
  now,

It is too late, too late.   How could I think

That you would wed, and never breathe a
  word!

[112]

And yet, I might have known, I might have
    known!
You have your father's will.

HUGH.

                  Ay, mother, words
Are naught to me but words: and all your
    words
Would never stay me when my heart was set.
If 'twas my father's way, I am his son.

ANN.

You are his son. Would, lad, that you were
    not!

HUGH.
Mother!

ANN.

      You're right, son, I will say no more.

I should have spoken then, or not at all.
It's now too late to speak.

ESTHER.
                          It's not too late.

HUGH, *slowly*.

Esther says truly. It's not yet too late.
You shall speak on now; it's too late to leave
Your thought unspoken, mother. You have
      said
Too much—too little to keep silence now.
The gate's unbarred; you cannot stay the
      flock.

ANN.

Have I not kept my counsel all these years?
Nay, I'll not speak now; it's too late, too late.
(*Turning to Esther.*)
Esther, my lass, I would you had not heard.

[114]

I wish you well, though you may doubt it
    now—
I wish you well with all my heart.   Come nigh
That I may kiss you.

ESTHER.
           It is not too late.
If you have any mercy in your heart,
Speak out your mind as though I were not
    here.

HUGH.
Ay, you shall speak out now.

ANN.
           Then I shall speak.
Maybe it's not too late.   I shall speak out
As I would one had spoken out to me
Upon my bridal-morn.   If my words seem
Too fierce, too bitter, it's because they spring

From a fierce, bitter heart. O Esther, lass,
'Twere better you should die than your young
　　heart
Grow old and fierce and bitter—better far
That it should break, and you should die,
　　than live
To grow old in black bitterness and wrath
As I have done. I have not much life left,
But I would save you, lass, with my last
　　breath,
If any word can fend off destiny.
And, Hugh, my son, though I speak bitter
　　things
To your unhappiness, I only seek
To snatch you from disaster. You have said
That words are weak: yet, I have nothing else.
You will not hate a poor, old woman, Hugh,
Because she snatches at a wisp of straw

To save the son who drowns before her eyes?
I must speak out the bitter, galling truth,
Though you should hate me, son, for ever-
    more.

HUGH.
Say on: I shall not hate you. Speak out all
If it will ease you.

ANN.
            Naught can bring me ease
Save death, and death bides long. Yet, I
    will speak.
You did not know your father, Hugh; he died
When you were in your cradle. You have
    heard
How, on a hurdle, he was brought home dead
From Thirlwall Crags; for folk have told you
    this,

Though I have never breathed his name to
  you.

They wondered how he fell. He did not fall.

And when I never spoke of him, they thought

That I was dumb with sorrow. It was hate

That held me mute. How should I mourn him
  dead

Whom I had hated living! Don't speak,
  Hugh,

Till I have told you all. Then you shall judge.

I scarce have breath to tell the tale; and yet,

'Twill soon be told; and if you hate me, son,

As I did hate your father, I fear not,

For I am too nigh death; and soon shall lie,

Unmindful of your hate as he of mine.

I could not hate you, son, although you bear

His name, and though his blood runs in your
  veins.

When first I knew him he was much like you—
As tall and broad and comely, and his eyes
The same fierce blue, his hair the same dull
    red.
Ay, you are like your father to your hands—
Your big, brown, cruel hands! You have his
    grip.
And he was just about your age; and lived
Here with his father, a fierce, silent man—
Mad Hugh the neighbours called him—whose
    wife died
Ere she could weary of her wedding-gown.
Folk said that fear had killed her. Yet, when
    Hugh,
Your father, wooed, I could not say him nay,
Though he was like his father. I was young,
And loved him for his very fierceness; proud
Because he was so big and strong; and yet,

I ever feared him; and, poor, trembling fool,
'Twas fear that drove me to him; and we
   wed
When old Hugh died. The day he brought
   me home—
Home to this self-same house, I shrank from
   him
Because I feared him, and he saw my fear.
I feared the passion in his wild, blue eyes,
And loathed his fiery love—so nigh to hate.
But I was his; and there was none to speak
As now I speak, or, on that very morn,
I should have left him. Ah, had I but known!
I was so young. A bitter year wore through,
And you were born, son: still I could not die,
Though fear was ever on me, and he knew
I feared him, and for that he hated me.
Have patience, lad; the tale is well-nigh told.

One day, when his hand touched me, I
    shrank back.

He saw, and sudden frenzy filled his eyes;

He clutched me by the throat with savage
    grip,

And flung me fiercely from him; and I fell

Against the hearthstone, and knew nothing
    more,

Till, coming to myself again, I found

That he was gone; and all the room was
    dark.

The night had fallen; and I heard you cry—

For you were in your cradle, Hugh—and
    rose,

Though all my body quivered with keen pain,

To suckle you. Next morn they brought
    him in,

Dead on a hurdle. When I swooned and fell,

They thought that grief had killed me; but, even then,

I could not die, and came to life again,

And wakened on this bed I have not left

So many years.   The folk were good to me,

And as they tended you I heard them talk,

And wonder how your father came to fall;

Yet, I spoke naught of him, because I knew

He hadn't fallen; but headlong to death

Had leapt, afraid his hand had murdered me.

Ay, panic drove him. . . .   You must hear me out.

Don't speak yet, lad.   I have not much to say.

But you are all your father!

HUGH.

I shall speak!

Say, mother, have I ever done you ill?

ANN.

No, son, you ever have been good to me,

Because I knew you, and I did not **fear**
you.

Yet, you are all your father. When a babe

I knew it, for your little fist would smite

The breast from which it fed in sudden wrath.

When you were barely weaned, a shepherd
brought

A poor, wee, motherless lamb for you to tend;

And though you loved it with your hot,
young heart,

And hugged it nigh to death; and, day or
night,

Would not be parted from it; yet one morn,

When it shrank from your fierce caress, your
hands

In sudden fury clutched its throat, and nigh

Had strangled it, ere it was snatched from
   you.
That day I vowed that you should never wed
If I might stay you. But I speak too late.
'Twere as much use to bid the unborn babe
Beware to breathe the bitter breath of life!

HUGH.

It is not yet too late. (*Turning to Esther.*)
                    Lass, you have heard.
(*Going to the door and throwing it open.*)
The door is open; you are free to go.
Why do you tarry? Are you not afraid?
Go, ere I hate you. I'll not hinder you.
I would not have you bound to me by fear.
Don't fear to leave me; rather fear to bide
With me who am my father's very son.
Go, lass, while yet I love you!

ESTHER, *closing the door.*

                              I shall bide.
I have heard all; and yet, I would not go,
Nor would I have a single word unsaid.
I loved you, husband; yet, I did not know you
Until your mother spoke. I know you now;
And I am not afraid.

(*Taking off her hat, and moving towards the table.*)

                    Come, take your seat.

THE SCAR

Persons:

ABEL FORSTER, a shepherd.

MARGARET FORSTER, his wife.

Scene: The Scar, a shepherd's cottage on the fells. Abel Forster is seated with his back to the open door, gazing with unseeing eyes into a smouldering peat-fire, the dull glow from which is the only light in the room. The pendulum of the hanging-clock is silent and motionless, and the choral voice of the moorland-burn and the intermittent hunting-cry of the owl are the only sounds that break the frosty silence of the night. Presently, a step is heard on the threshold, and Margaret Forster enters, wrapped in a shawl which covers the bundle

[126]

*she is carrying in her arms. As she sinks
wearily into a chair by the door, Abel looks up
at her, uncertainly; then fixes his eyes again
on the fire, from which he does not raise them
while speaking.*

ABEL.
So, you are back!

MARGARET.
                        Yes, I am back.
ABEL.
                                    I knew,
Sooner or later, you would come again.
I have expected you these many nights,
But thought to see you sooner, lass.

MARGARET.
                              And yet,
You could not know: I did not know myself;
And even at the door I almost turned.

ABEL.

Yet, you are here.

MARGARET.

Yes, I am here to-night;
But where the dawn shall find me I don't
know.

ABEL.

You would not go again! Lass, do you think
My door shall ever stand ajar for you
To come and go when it may please your
whim?

MARGARET.

No; if I go again, I don't come back.

ABEL.

You shall not go.

MARGARET.

       Ah! have you not learned aught

From the long months that taught so much
    to me?

ABEL.

Ay, lass, I have learned something. Do not
    leave me.

You, too, have learned, you say; and have
    come home.

Why go again into the world to starve

While there is food and shelter for you
    here?

But you will bide. We shall forget the past.

Let us forgive each other. . . .

MARGARET.

              I don't come

To crave forgiveness—nor would I forget.

ABEL.

Why have you come then? Were you hunger-
     driven?

O lass, I hoped . . .

MARGARET.

                    No, I don't come to beg;

Nor would I starve while I have hands to
     work.

I lacked nor food nor shelter since I left.

ABEL.

Then, why have you returned?

MARGARET.

                    I have come back

Because I am the mother of your son.

(*She rises from her seat and throws back her
shawl, revealing a baby at her breast.*)

[130]

ABEL, *looking up.*

My son! Ah, Margaret!   Now I understand.
To think I didn't know!

MARGARET.

The boy was born
A month ago.

ABEL.

Your babe has brought you home.
You will not go again.   You have come back
Because you could not quite forget!

MARGARET.

I've come
Because the babe is yours.   I would not keep
Your own from you; nor would I rob the child
Of home and father.

ABEL.

Had you no other thought?

[131]

Had you forgotten in so brief a while
How we had loved, lass?

MARGARET.
                    We knew naught of love.

ABEL.
Did we not know love when we wedded?

MARGARET.
                                    Nay;
We knew not love. In passion we were wed;
And passion parted us as easily.

ABEL.
Ay, passion parted us. Yet, surely, love
Brings us again together. We were young
And hasty, maybe, when we wed; but, lass,
I have awaited these seven weary months
For your return; and with the sheep by
    day,

Or brooding every night beside the hearth,
I have thought long on many things. The
    months
Have brought me wisdom; and I love. I
    knew
You would return; for you, too, have found
    love.

MARGARET.
Is this your wisdom? Little have you learned.
You are as hasty as the day we wed!
I, too, have brooded long on many things.
Maybe, my wisdom is no more than yours,
But only time will tell. Who knows! I've
    lived
And laboured in the city these long months;
And though I found friends even there, and
    folk

Were good to me; and, when the boy was
    born,
A neighbour tended me—yet, to my heart,
The city was a solitude; I lived
Alone in all that teeming throng of folk.
Yet, I was not afraid to be alone;
Nor, in my loneliness, did I regret
That we had parted; for the solitude
Revealed so much that else I had not learned
Of my own heart to me. But, when, at length
I knew another life within me stirred,
My thoughts turned homewards to the hills; it
    seemed
So pitiful that a baby should be born
Amid that stifling squalor. As I watched
The little children, starved and pinched and
    white,
Already old in evil ere their time,

Who swarmed in those foul alleys, and who
    played
In every gutter of the reeking courts,
I vowed no child of mine should draw its
    breath
In that dark city, by our waywardness
Robbed of the air and sun, ay, and the hills,
And the wide playground of the windy heath:
And yet, I lingered till the boy was born.
But, as he nestled at my breast, he drew
The angry pride from me; and, as I looked
Upon him I remembered you. He brought
Me understanding; and his wide, blue eyes
Told me that he was yours; and, while he
    slept,
I often lay awake and thought of you;
And wondered what life held for this wee babe.
And sometimes in the night . . .

ABEL.

Have you, too, known
The long night-watches?   Since you went
away,
Each morning, as I left the lonely house,
My heart said: surely she will come to-day;
And when each evening I returned from toil,
I looked to meet you on the threshold; yet,
By night alone within the silent house
I longed for you the sorest.   Through lone
hours
My heart has listened for your step, until
I trembled at the noises of the night.
I am no craven, yet, the moor-owl's shriek
At midnight, or the barking of a fox,
Or even the drumming of the snipe ere dawn
Has set me quaking.   Ay, night long, for you
The door was left ajar.   And, hour by hour,

I've listened to the singing of the burn
Until I had each tinkling note by heart.
Though I have lived my life among the hills,
I never listened to a stream before.
Yet, little comfort all its melody
Could bring my heart; but now that you are
    back
It seems to sing you welcome to your home.
You have come home. You could not quite
    forget.

MARGARET.
I have forgotten naught; and naught I rue:
Yet, when the weakness left me, I arose
To bring your babe to you.

ABEL.

               Naught but the babe?

MARGARET.

Lad, shut the door; for I am cold; and fetch
Some peats to mend the fire; it's almost out.
You need a woman's hand to tend you, lad.
See, you have let the clock run down!

ABEL.

My heart
Kept bitter count of all those lonely hours.
Margaret, your wisdom is no less than mine;
And mine is love, lass.

MARGARET.

Only time will tell.

WINTER DAWN

Persons:

STEPHEN REED, a shepherd.

ELIZABETH REED, Stephen's wife.

MARY REED, Stephen's mother.

Scene: Callersteads, a lonely shepherd's cottage on the fells. A candle burns on the window-sill, though the light of dawn already glimmers through the snow-blinded panes. Elizabeth Reed paces the sanded floor with impatient step. Mary Reed sits crouched on the settle over the peat-fire; Elizabeth's baby sleeping in a cradle by her side.

ELIZABETH.

The men are long away.

[139]

MARY.

                Have patience, lass;

They'll soon be back; they've scarce been
    gone an hour.

It's toilsome travelling when the drifts are
    deep;

And William is no longer young. Fear
    naught,

They'll bring back Stephen with them safe
    and sound.

ELIZABETH.

You know he could not live through such a
    night.

MARY.

Nay, none may know but God. I only know

That I have heard my father many times

Tell over and over, as though it were some
    tale
He'd learned by heart—for he was innocent
And helpless as a babe for many years
Before death took him—how, when he was
    young,
A hundred sheep were buried in the drifts
Down Devil's Sike, yet not an ewe was lost,
Though five days passed ere they could be
    dug out;
And they had cropped the grass beneath
    their feet
Bare to the roots, and nibbled at their wool
To stay the pangs of hunger, when, at last,
The shepherds found them, nearly starved,
    poor beasts.
If the frost hold, sheep live for many days
Beneath a drift; the snow lies on them light,

So they can draw their breath, and keep them
    warm;
But when the thaw comes it is death to them,
For they are smothered 'neath the melting
    snow.
I've heard my father speak these very words
A thousand times; and I can see him now,
As, huddled in the ingle o'er the fire,
With crazy eyes and ever-groping hands,
He sat all day, and mumbled to himself.
If silly sheep can keep themselves alive
So many days and nights, a shepherd lad,
With all his wits to strive against the storm,
Would never perish in a day and night;
And Stephen is a man. . . .

ELIZABETH.

                  If Stephen lived,

He would not bide from home a day and
    night;
He could not lose his way across the fell,
Unless the snow o'ercame him.

MARY.
                    Yet, maybe,
He sheltered 'neath a dyke, and fell asleep;
And William and his man will find him there.

ELIZABETH.
Ay, they will find him sleeping sure enough,
But from that slumber who shall waken him?

MARY.
Nay, lass, you shall not speak so! Stephen
    lives,
The mother's heart within me tells me this:
That I shall look upon my son again
Before an hour has passed.

ELIZABETH.

A wife's love knows

Its loss ere it be told; and in my heart

I know this night has taken him from me.

My husband's eyes shall never look again

In mine, nor his lips ever call me wife.

You cannot love him as I love him. . . .

MARY.

Lass!

ELIZABETH.

Because he is your son, you love him, woman;

But I, for love of him, became his bride.

MARY.

Lass, don't speak so. Your son cries out to
you.

Take him within your arms, and comfort him

Until his father comes.

[144]

ELIZABETH.

            Poor babe, poor babe!

Your father nevermore will look on you,

And hug you to his breast, and call you his.

Nay! shut your eyes!

      (*To Mary.*) O woman, take the boy!

I cannot bear to look into those eyes

So like his father's! Hark! did you hear

    aught?

MARY.

Someone is on the threshold. See who comes.

ELIZABETH.

No! No! I dare not. Give me back the child,

And open you the door. Quick, woman,

    quick!

Surely strange fingers fumble at the latch!

(*As she speaks, the door slowly opens, and*

Stephen enters wearily, with faltering step, and groping like a blind man. Elizabeth runs to meet him, but he passes her unseeing, and walks towards the hearth.)

ELIZABETH.

Stephen! (*Shrinking as he passes her.*) It
    is not he!

MARY.
             My son! My son!

STEPHEN, *speaking slowly and wearily.*

Ay, mother, are you there? I cannot see you.

Why have you lit no candle? Fetch a light.

This darkness hurts my eyes. I scarce could
    find

The track across the fell. Did you forget

To set the candle on the window-sill?

Or maybe 'twas the snow that hid the flame.

The master kept me late, because my task
Was but half-done; and, when I left the school,
The snow was deep, and blew into my eyes,
Pricking them like hot needles. I was tired,
And hardly could win home, it was so dark;
Yet, that strange darkness burned mine eyes
    like fire,
And dazzled them like flame, and still they
    burn.
But why do you sit lightless? Fetch a light,
That I may see. It must be very late.
I seemed to wander through an endless night;
And I am weary and would go to bed.

MARY.

Son, sit you down. The snow has blinded you.
You will see better soon.

      (Handing him a pot from the hob.)

                Come, drink this ale;

It's hot, and will put life in your cold limbs.

Your supper awaits you; you are very late.

(*To Elizabeth.*)

Lass, speak a word to him!

ELIZABETH.

                It is not he!

MARY.

Ay, lass, it's he. The snow's bewildered him;

He dreams he is a little lad again.

But speak you to him; he will know your
      voice.

Your word may call his wits again to him.

ELIZABETH.

No! No! The night has taken him from me.

This is not he who went out yesterday,

My kiss upon his lips, to seek the sheep,

And bring them into shelter from the storm.
My husband's eyes shall never look in mine
Again, nor his lips ever call me wife.
This is not he!

STEPHEN.

        Why do you bring no light?
The darkness hurts my eyes. Do you not
    heed?
I never knew such darkness. It is strange,
I feel the glow, yet cannot see the peats.

MARY.

Lass, speak a word!

ELIZABETH.

       Stephen! . . . He doesn't hear me.

STEPHEN.

Whom do you speak with, mother? Is father
    back

Already from the mart? But I forget—
It must be late; 'twas dark ere I left school—
So strangely dark; it scorched my eyes like
    fire.

MARY.

Son, don't you know Elizabeth?

STEPHEN.

                    The lass
With big, brown eyes who sits by me at school?
Ay, ay, I know her well; but what of her?

MARY.

Do you not know Elizabeth, your wife?

STEPHEN.

Mother, I am too weary for your jest;
And my eyes hurt me. I would go to sleep.
Light me to bed. Why do you bring no light?

MARY.

Ah, God, that he had slept to wake no more!

ELIZABETH.

What say you, woman? Have you not your
    son?
It's I have lost my husband, and my babe
Is fatherless.

MARY.
                No, he may know the babe!
You take the boy and lay him in his lap.
Maybe his child will bring him to himself.
Son, do you not remember your poor babe?

STEPHEN.

My baby brother, Philip? But he died
So long ago; what makes you speak of him?
Yes, I remember well the day he died,
And how the snow fell when they buried him.

The mare could scarce make headway through
    the drifts,
And plunged and stumbled, and the cart sank
    oft
Over the axle-tree; and when, at last,
We reached the church, the storm closed in
    again,
And happed the little coffin in white flakes,
Ere they had laid it in the grave. To-night
'Twas such a storm. I must have lost my
    way,
The night has seemed so long, and I am
    tired.
Mother, a light! The darkness hurts my eyes.
You do not heed.

MARY.
               At least you know me, son!
God give you light, ay! even though it blind

Your eyes to me for ever, so that you
May know your wife and child!

ELIZABETH.
                                        My little babe!
He has forgotten us and does not love us.
The cruel night has taken him from us.
Don't cry, my son. He'll pay no heed to
    you.
Last night your father and my husband died.

STEPHEN.
I am so weary, mother. Bring a light.

MARY.
Son, take my hand. I'll lead you to your
    bed.
Maybe, a healing sleep will make you whole,
And bring your wandering spirit home again.
[153]

ELIZABETH.

No, no! It's I must lead him! He is mine.

The night has taken my husband, but the
dawn

Has brought him back, a helpless child, to
me.

He fumbles in the darkness; yet, my love

Shall be a light to lead him to the end.

Come, Stephen, take my hand.

STEPHEN.

Elizabeth!

What are you doing from home on such a
night?

You have a gentle touch; I'll come with you.

It seems the snow has blinded me; but you

Will lead me safely through this dazzling
dark.

Come, lass, for I am weary, and would sleep.

[154]

MARY, *as Elizabeth and Stephen pass out of
the room.*

Ay, you must lead him to the end. Though
    sleep
May heal his sight, it cannot heal his mind,
Or lift the deeper darkness from his soul.
My poor, old father lives again in him;
And he, my son, so young and hale, must
    tread
The twilight road to death. Ah God! Ah
    God!
Through me the curse has fallen on my son!
Yet, when the madness on my father fell,
He was a frail, old man, and nigher death;
And Stephen is so young and full of life.
Nay! Surely, it's the storm has stricken
    him!
Elizabeth, your poor heart spoke too true:

[155]

The bitter night has widowed you, your babe
Is fatherless, and you must lead my son
Through the bewildering dark. But yesterday
It seems I guided his first baby steps!
Ay, you must lead him; you are young and strong,
And I am old and feeble, and my hand
Would fail him ere he reached the journey's end.

(*The baby cries out, and Mary takes him in her arms.*)

Poor babe, poor babe! A bleak dawn breaks for you!

(*A sound of footsteps on the threshold.*)

The seekers are returning. William comes;
And I must tell him that his son is home.

[156]

THE FERRY

Persons:

JOHN TODD, an old ferryman.

ROBERT TODD, his son.

JANE TODD, Robert's wife.

*Scene: The living room of the ferry-house—
a door opening on to the river-bank, another
to the inner room. It is evening in early spring,
and the ceaseless roar of the river in flood
sounds through the room. John, seated at a
cobbler's bench, works by candle-light. Jane,
coming from the inner room, takes a chair to
the fireside, and sits down with her knitting.
The outer door opens, and Robert enters.*

ROBERT.

The river's in full-spate.

[157]

JANE.

Ay, how it roars!

JOHN, *looking up from his work.*
The snow has melted on the fells.

JANE.

That wind
Will puff the candle out. Lad, shut the door.

JOHN.
It's fresh, and smells of spring. 'Twas such
  a night. . .

ROBERT.
Wife, I'll away down to the Traveller's Rest.

JANE.
Well, don't be late.

JOHN.

But what about the boat?

ROBERT.

The boat is safe enough; I've made her fast.

JOHN.

Ay, lad, but what if anyone should hail,

And you not here to answer to their call?

I cannot take the oars; you know that well.

ROBERT.

The devil himself could never cross to-night;

The water is too big.   (*Goes out.*)

JOHN.
                          'Twas such a night

That Margaret hailed, and did not hail in
    vain.

I did not fear the flood.

JANE.
                          You cannot hear

How loud it roars. Your ears are dull with
    age.
You could not cross to-night.

JOHN.
                    If Margaret called,
Old as I am, I'd take the oars my hands
Have touched not these long years. If
    Margaret called—
But she will call no more. (*Bends over his
    work.*)

JANE.
                    You could not cross.

JOHN.
I would that Robert had not gone to-night.

JANE.
Why, he's a steady lad; there's little harm.

JOHN.

Ay, lass; and yet, I wish he had not gone.

If anyone should hail, and he not here!

JANE.

No one will hail to-night.

JOHN.

                'Twas such a night

That Margaret hailed.

JANE.

            'Twas cruel madness then.

JOHN.

She knew that I would come.

JANE.

                 More shame to her

That she should call you to nigh-certain
    death!

JOHN.

How can you speak of Robert's mother so!

She knew my arm was strong. She came that
    night

Home from the city, after many years.

She stood upon the bank and called my name,

And I, above the roar of waters, heard,

And took the oars and crossed to her, though
    twice

The river caught me in its swirl, and strove

To sweep me to the dam. But I was strong,

And reached the other bank; and in she
    stepped,

And never seemed to think of fear. Her eyes

Were on me, and I rowed her home, though
    death

Clutched at the boat, and sought to drag us
    down;

For I was young and strong. That May we
    wed;

And by the next spring-floods the boy was
    born,

And she lay dead—and I, so young and
    strong!

My strength that brought her through the
    roaring spate

Could not hold back that silent-ebbing life.

      (Bends over his work.)

JANE.

Yes, I have heard the story many times.

*(Silence falls on the room save for the roar of the
river. After a while, John lifts his head as
though listening.)*

JOHN.

Hark! What is that?

JANE.

It's nothing but the flood.

JOHN, *still listening.*
She calls!

JANE.

Who calls?

JOHN.

Do you hear naught?

JANE.

Nay, naught.
There's naught to hear—only the river's roar.
(*John bends again over his work, and is silent
for a while; but often lifts his head as though
listening. At last he speaks.*)

JOHN.
Can you hear naught, lass? Someone hails
the boat.

JANE.

It's but your fancy. How could you hear aught
With your deaf ears, when I can scarcely catch
My needles' click—the river roars so loud!

JOHN.

I heard a voice.

JANE.

          I tell you it was naught.
No voice could cross that flood. If any called,
That roar would drown their cry. You could
    not hear.
But no one would be fool enough to call
On such a night as this.

JOHN.

          I heard a voice.
I would that Robert had not gone to-
    night. . . .

JANE.

What could he do if he were here?

JOHN.

                        I crossed

On such a night.

JANE.

             Ay, ay, but Robert's wed.

JOHN, *starting up.*

Hark, hark, she calls! I hear the voice again.

JANE, *rising and laying a hand on his arm.*

Nay, father! Sit thee down. There's no one
    calls.

Your memory tricks you. It's the river's roar

That rings in your old head, and mazes you.

    (*John sits down again at his bench.*)

It sounds as though it sought to drag the banks

Along with it—and all! You'd almost think
That it was round the house!
  (*Goes to the door and opens it and looks out.*)
                          How fierce and black
Among the rocks it threshes 'neath the moon!
It makes me shudder though we're high and
    dry.
                          (*Closes the door.*)
JOHN.
Did you see no one on the other bank?

JANE.
No one was there to see. Who should there
    be?
(*John bends again over his work; then stops, and
sits gazing into the fire, still listening.*)

JOHN, *rising and speaking slowly.*
Lass, someone hails the boat; and I must go,
For Robert is not here.

JANE, *rising too, and holding him by the arm as he turns towards the door.*

You go! You go!
What would you do, you poor, old crazy man?
'Twould break you like a straw!

JOHN.

Yes, I am old;
But Robert is not here.

JANE.

If he were here
He could do naught. The flood would crush the boat
Like any eggshell!

JOHN.

Robert should be here.
Hark, hark, the voice again! Lass, I must go.
(*He tries to move towards the door, but Jane*

takes him by the arms and forces him back into his seat.)

JANE.

You crazed, old man! Sit down. What
would you do?

You need not hurry to your death; fear not,

'Twill come ere you are ready! Sit you
down.

You're feeble in my hands as any babe.

What could you do against that raging flood?

JOHN.

Yes, I am weak, who once was young and
strong.

But Robert should be here.

JANE.

I'll fetch him home.

If you'll sit quiet till I come again.

(*John gazes silently into the fire, then closes his eyes as if asleep.*)

JANE.

He's quiet now; the silly fit has passed.

Yet, I will go for Robert. It were best

That he should come. I think I should go
    crazed

Betwixt the flood and his fond, doting talk.

I fear I don't know what. It's that old man

Has filled me with his fancies; but he sleeps

Sound as a babe. I'll go for Robert now,

And be back ere he wakes.

(*Throws a shawl over her head, and goes out softly, closing the door behind her. John sits for a while with his eyes still shut; then starts up suddenly, and stands listening.*)

[170]

JOHN.

She calls! She calls!

(*Moves to the door and throws it open.*)

I come! I come!

(*Shading his eyes with his hand and gazing into the night.*) She awaits me on the
bank,

Beyond the raging waters, in the light.

Margaret, I come!

(*He goes out, leaving the door open. The clank of a chain being unloosed is heard; then nothing save the thresh of the river. Some moments pass; then voices are heard on the threshold.*)

ROBERT, *outside.*

The door is open, lass.

You should not leave it so.

JANE, *entering*.

I shut it close.

Father! He is not here! He's gone!

ROBERT.

Gone where?

JANE.

Robert, the boat! the boat! (*They rush out together.*)

ROBERT, *his voice heard above the roar of the waters*.

The boat's gone too! Quick, to the dam!

JANE, *as they pass the door*.

He seemed to sleep so sound.

(*The candle gutters out in the draught from the open door, and nothing is heard but the noise of the waters.*)

[172]

ON THE THRESHOLD

Persons:

PHILIP RIDLEY, a young shepherd.

ALICE RIDLEY, his bride.

ELLEN HALL, an elderly woman.

Scene: Cragshields, a cottage on the fells. Through a little window to one side of the hearth a far-off lough is seen, glittering in the April sunshine. Now and again, the call of the curlew is heard. Philip Ridley and his wife are seated at breakfast near the open door.

ALICE.

No more of love, lad! We are wedded folk
With work to do, and little time enough
To earn our bread in; and must put away
Such lovers' folly.

[173]

PHILIP.

> Can you say so, lass,

Hearing the curlew pipe down every slack!

Their mating-call runs rippling through my
   blood.

Hark, do you hear how shrill and sweet it is!

Does it stir naught in you? You have no
   heart

If that can leave you cold which thrills me
   through

Till every vein's a-tingle.

ALICE.

> Shut the door,

And sup your porridge ere it cools. You
   know

Even the curlew cannot live on love.

He's a wise bird, and soon will sober down.

He courts but in due season, and his voice

[174]

Keeps not the wooing note the whole year
    long.

So must we settle down, lad. Do you think

Old William Hall and his goodwife who
    dwelt,

For sixty years, together in this house,

Before our coming, as the neighbours tell,

Lived like young lovers through so many
    years?

PHILIP.

But we've not mated, lass, as curlew mate;

Our love shall know no season. I have heard

That William and his wife were hard and
    cold,

And seldom spoke save with a bitter tongue.

ALICE.

And yet, they dwelt beneath this very roof

Together sixty years—as we may dwell!
They must have wed as young as we, and
    come
Home to this hearth as full of foolish hope.
I shudder when I think of those long years.

PHILIP.
Don't think of them, for they are naught to
    you.

ALICE.
Had they no children, then?

PHILIP.
                But one, a lass;
And she was led astray. They cast her out,
And barred the door upon her one wild night;
And what became of her none ever knew.
The neighbours ne'er heard tell of her again.

ALICE.

I wonder if she lives, poor soul! And yet,

I'd bar the door on any child of mine. . . .

PHILIP.

You wouldn't, Alice. You don't know your
    heart.

We'll speak no more of them. The past is
    past,

And throws no shadow on our lives; no ghost

Of old unhappiness shall haunt our home.

The years hold no such bitterness for us;

And naught shall come between us and our
    love.

ALICE.

Now you are at your foolish talk! It's time

That you were with the sheep. If you have
    naught

To turn your hand to, I have more to do

Than may be done ere bedtime. Shift your
　　seat

Till I have cleared the table, lad.

PHILIP.
　　　　　　　　　　　No, lass,

I must away; but, ere I go, one kiss

To keep my heart up through the morning!

ALICE.
　　　　　　　　　　　　　　　Go,

You foolish lad! You're still a boy.

PHILIP.
　　　　　　　　　　　　　Time mends

The folly that is youth—if it be folly

To live and love in happiness and hope;

For we are young but once; and, as you say,

We have full sixty years in which to grow

Wise, cold and crabbed, if we should live as
    long
As William and his wife.

       (*To his collie.*) Down, Nelly, down!
I will be back ere noonday.

    (*Goes out, closing the door behind him.*)

ALICE.
                        Sixty years!
It's a long while to dwell in bitterness.
I wonder if they ever loved as we
When they were young. Maybe they did,
    until
Their daughter's trouble soured their hearts
    —and yet,
Surely, if they had loved! . . . Ah, well,
    the years
Must bring what they will bring, and we abide
The winter, though it freeze the springs of love.

[179]

(*She turns to her work of scrubbing and sweep-
ing. After a while, the door opens noiselessly;
and Ellen Hall stands on the threshold, unseen
to Alice who is bending over the hearth.*)

ELLEN, *gazing about her absently.*
The dresser stood against the other wall.
(*Seeing Alice, who looks up suddenly in amaze-
ment.*)
Forgive me that I did not knock. So long
I raised this latch a dozen times a day,
Undreaming that the hour would ever
  come
When I should need to knock, that, when,
  once more,
I stood upon the threshold, I forgot
The years that stood between me and my
  home,

[180]

And that I came a stranger to this house.
Forgive me. . . .

ALICE.
      Nay, come in, and take a seat.
We are newcomers to these parts. . . .

ELLEN.
                Had you
Been born and bred within a mile or so,
You would not know me, lass; for you are
     young;
And it is forty years since I left home.
But you shall know me ere I take a seat
Beneath your roof. If you will ask me
     then. . . .
You start at that! I see that you have heard
My tale already. I am Ellen Hall,
The outcast whom the neighbours told you of.

But I must go.   Forgive me that I brought
My shadow in your house.   I meant no harm.
I only wished to see my home once more.

ALICE.
Nay, nay, come in, and rest; for you are tired.
You must not go with neither bite nor sup.
I'll set the kettle on the bar. . . .

ELLEN.
                                        Nay, lass,
I will not eat nor drink, but I would rest
A little while, for my old feet have found
The fell-road long and heavy, though my heart
Grew young again, breathing the upland air.
Let me not hinder you: just do your work
As though I were not here.   I'll not bide long.
(*After a pause.*)
Lass, do you love your man?

ALICE.

I wedded him.

ELLEN.

Though your reproof be bitter, it is just;
But I have lived so long on bitter words
That I, long since, have lost the taste of them.
I did not speak the word in wantonness;
For as I look upon you where you stand
In your fresh bloom of youth, old memories
    stir
Within me; for your eyes are kind. My heart
That has not spoken out so many years
A moment longed to tell its tale to you,
The tale it never told to any heart;
But it shall keep its silence to the end,
For you are proud and happy in your youth,
As I was proud and happy once. Ay, lass,
Even I was young and comely in my time—

Though you may smile to hear it now, as then
I should have smiled. . . . Nay, lass, I do
    not blame you!
Forgive a lonely woman, frail and old,
Whom years and grief have brought to foolish-
    ness.

ALICE.
Nay, nay, I didn't smile. I'd hear your tale
If you would tell it me. 'Twill ease your
    heart
To pour its sorrow in another's ear.
But if you would keep silence, breathe no
    word.
Yet, bide till you are rested.

ELLEN.
                Thank you, lass.

A silence that has lasted forty years

May not be broken in a breathing space.

It isn't easy, speaking; yet, I'll speak

Because your eyes are kind, and nevermore

Shall look upon me when the tale is told.

I haven't much to tell, for you have heard

The neighbours' talk; and yet, lass, none may
know

The heart's true story save the heart itself;

And they who speak, not knowing the full
truth,

May twist on idle tongues unwittingly

What little of the truth is theirs. You know

It was my sin, as folk account it sin,

To love beyond my station—ay, to love

Unquestioning, undoubting, unafraid—

To love with the fierce faith and simple might

And courage of a young girl's innocence,

In sweet, blind trustfulness and happy pride,

[185]

As many a maid has loved, nor lived to rue.

Yet, I don't blame him: he was passion's
fool—

Ay, one of those from whom hard fate with-
holds

The wonder and the tenderness of love—

Though I believed he loved me as I loved,

And as I love him yet—ay, even yet!

Blindly I loved him—blinded by the light

Of my own love, my love that still. . . But
you,

Unless you love, you will not understand;

For only love brings knowledge. You have
heard

How, when he left me, I was turned from
home.

Abandoned in my trouble, I was thrust

On the cold mercy of a winter night.

This very door was barred against my woe—
I still can hear that bolt shot after me—
Although I never turned. Nay, speak no
    word!
I crave no pity; for I loved, and love
Brooks no compassion from a happier heart.
And I remember little of that night;
It scarcely seemed to matter when so much
Was gone from me that all should go. To me
My parents had ever been shrewd and harsh
As to each other. They had never known
The tenderness of love; for they had wed
In wanton passion which had left them cold,
To live for sixty years on bitter words,
For they were over eighty when both died,
As though they had been lovers, on one
    day.
Spare all the fresh young pity of your heart

For those whom chance has tethered with-
   out love
To tread together the same patch of life
Till death release them.

ALICE.
                Did you ne'er return?

ELLEN.
Love's outcasts don't come back.

ALICE.
                Might not the years
Have softened their hard hearts? They would
   relent. . .

ELLEN.
Time brings no understanding without love;
Love cannot spring from barrenness; the soil
That does not quicken to the breath of spring
Will bear no blade of green in winter days.

I pitied them; and, had my child but lived,
I had forgiven them with all my heart.

ALICE.

Ah! they were cruel! but you, what could you
    do?

ELLEN.

I lived—but not as idle tongues have lied.
I loved him, lass; and if your heart is true
To love, 'twill know that I speak truly. Yet,
What can the happy know of love! O lass,
You are too fresh and fair to have known
    love!

ALICE.
Yet, I love Philip.

ELLEN.

                    Nay, you cannot love!

They don't know love who have not starved
    for love,
And worked their fingers to the bone for
    love,
And lived for love, without love's recom-
    pense,
Death holding within easy reach the while
The escape and solace of forgetfulness.
Still, you may love—for, even unto me,
Love once was happiness. Forgive me, lass;
It is so long since I knew happiness.
You have not idle hands; but then you
    toil
For him you love and who loves you again,
While I have laboured only for my love
Of him who never loved me, unto whom
I was a broken trinket, cast aside,
Forgotten, for he wedded years ago.

Forgive me, if I weary you; so long

My heart has brooded in its solitude

On all these things, oft shaping them to
words

For its own comfort—for even words give
ease

To aching and intolerable thought—

Although it could not utter them aloud,

That, now they find a vent, they teem, a
spate

Enough to drown your patience.

ALICE.

                        Nay, speak on.

ELLEN.

I have dwelt long in grey and narrow streets,

A stranger among strangers, where men
snatch

A starveling living from each other's clutch;

[191]

Ay, I have toiled in cities where men grind
Their brothers' bones for bread, where life
    is naught
But labour and starvation to the end.
Lass, may your kind eyes never need to grow,
As mine have grown, accustomed to the sight
Of the evil and the wretchedness and want
That huddle in dark alleys; yet even there
Love shines, though cooped in stifling misery,
A candle in a garret. To the poor,
Life is not easy underneath the sun,
But in the dark and reeking city ways
It's more relentless, grim and terrible—
The endless struggle. Lass, I never thought
To look upon the hills of home again,
Or tread the ling, or breathe the living air
That I had breathed, a heedless child; but
    when

By chance I heard my parents both were gone
To where the shadow of a daughter's shame
Might never vex their slumber, my heart
    yearned
To gaze once more o'er the familiar fells
Where I had first found love. So I set out,
Hoping to come and go ere the new herd
Should take possession. As I crossed the
    crags,
I saw the smoke curl o'er the chimney-stack,
And knew I came too late.

ALICE.
                Nay, not too late!
You have not come too late!

ELLEN.
                I nigh turned back.
I had not meant to cross the threshold-stone;
[193]

But as I climbed the brae-top, and looked
    forth
Over the sweep of bent and heath, and
    breathed
The morning air, and gazed upon the loughs
A-shimmer in the sun, and heard the call
Of curlew down the slacks, and felt the spring
Of heather under-foot, I—who had thought
So little of these things when I had lived,
A careless lass, among them, but had come
To hanker after them in city streets—
Was filled with strange forgetfulness, and
    moved
As in a trance, scarce knowing what I did,
Till I had raised the latch, and saw your
    eyes
In wonder fixed on mine. But I must go
Before your man comes in.

ALICE.

               No, you must bide.
This is your home. You must not go again
Back to the city. You are old and weak;
And I and Philip are both young and strong
To work for you, if you will live with us.

ELLEN.

With all my heart I thank you, lass, and yet,
I may not bide. Though I am old and weak,
I would tread out my pathway to the end.
It is too late, too late to turn aside;
Nor would I if I could, since I have fared
So far along the solitary way.
I could not rest at ease in idleness.
Yet, I shall go to take up work again
With kindlier memories of my home, and
      when

Once more the narrow alleys on me close,

I shall remember someone living here

Whom love has given understanding. Life

Be good to you—yes, I can wish you
    this,

Though you have all that life withheld from
    me.

I don't know what the future holds, and
    yet,

Whatever may befall you, this is sure:

You shall not know the utmost bitterness;

Life cannot be all barren, having love.

From the full knowledge of my heart I speak

As one who through the perilous night has
    come

To you, upon the threshold of your day,

The dawnlight on your brow. Lass, fare
    you well!

ALICE.

Farewell! and yet, I grieve that you should
go

Back to the struggle who have brought to
me

The secret you have wrung from life.

(*Kissing her.*)   Farewell!

You have revealed to me my happiness.

ELLEN.

Your kiss brings comfort, daughter.   Fare
you well!

(*She goes out, and Alice stands in the doorway,
gazing after her for a while.   Presently a gate
clashes hard by, and Philip approaches.*)

PHILIP.

What do you look on, lass—so rare a light

Burns in your deep, brown eyes! What do
    you see?
Have you been listening to the curlew's call?

ALICE.

No: I have heard a voice from out the past;
And my eyes look down all the happy years
That you and I must travel, side by side.

Printed in the United States of America

Daily Bread

New Edition. Three volumes in one. Cloth, 12mo, $1.25

"A Millet in word-painting who writes with a terrible simplicity is Wilfrid Wilson Gibson, born in Hexham, England, in 1878, of whom Canon Cheyne wrote: 'A new poet of the people has risen up among us.' The story of a soul is written as plainly in 'Daily Bread' as in 'The Divine Comedy' and in 'Paradise Lost.'"—*The Outlook*.

Fires

Cloth, 12mo, $1.25

"In 'Fires' as in 'Daily Bread,' the fundamental note is human sympathy with the whole of life. Impressive as these dramas are, it is in their cumulative effect that they are chiefly powerful."—*Atlantic Monthly*.

THE MACMILLAN COMPANY
Publishers   64–66 Fifth Avenue   New York

Songs and Satires

By EDGAR LEE MASTERS, Author of "Spoon River
Anthology"

Cloth, 12mo.

No book of recent years had made the sensation in
poetry circles that followed the appearance of Mr.
Masters's *Spoon River Anthology*. Comparatively un-
known prior to its publication, Mr. Masters was soon
the most discussed writer in America and his volume
was called by many critics, W. S. Braithwaite among
others, the most important contribution to letters of
1915. This has stimulated interest in his new collec-
tion, in which will be found exhibited again those
qualities of imagination, of originality, of humor, which
brought success to its predecessor.

The Great Maze—The Heart of Youth: A Poem and a Play

By HERMAN HAGEDORN, Author of "Poems and Bal-
lads," "Faces in the Dawn," etc.

Cloth, 12mo.

In this book are contained two remarkable pieces
of work which show conclusively Mr. Hagedorn's
ability in distinctly different fields. *The Great Maze*
is a long poem concerned with the murder of Agamem-
non by Ægisthus and the events leading up to this
catastrophe. It is finely conceived and Clytemnestra's
gradual revolt against Ægisthus and her sudden sur-
render to the love of her husband put new and whole-
some life into a tale that is dramatic of itself. *The
Heart of Youth*, on the other hand, is a play presenting
a picture of youth with all its buoyancy, and love of
freedom, and exhibiting to the full the author's power
of expression and imagination.

THE MACMILLAN COMPANY
Publishers   64–66 Fifth Avenue   New York